Earlybirds, Earlywords

Pictures and verse by Ann & Roger Bonner

Scroll Press

New York

First U.S. publication 1973 by Scroll Press Inc.
ISBN: 0-87592-013-6

Bare trees
Rising sun
Winter colors
Each one

Hens ruffle
Cocks crow
Breeze stirs
Dawn glow

Black bird
Brown thrush
Welcomes day
From every bush

Sleepy dog
In the straw
Blinks an eye
Moves a paw

Gentle cow
With coat of silk
Mooing softly
Gives her milk

Glassy puddles
Iron sky
First bus
Rumbles by

Electric cart
Happy hum
Crates rattle
Milk's come

Windowlight
Sunshine
Another day
All mine

Paper boy
Opens gate
Breakfast news
By the plate

Bacon smell
Drifting round
Sizzles crackles
Hungry sound

Chimney smoke
Frosty street
Crystal breath
Frozen feet

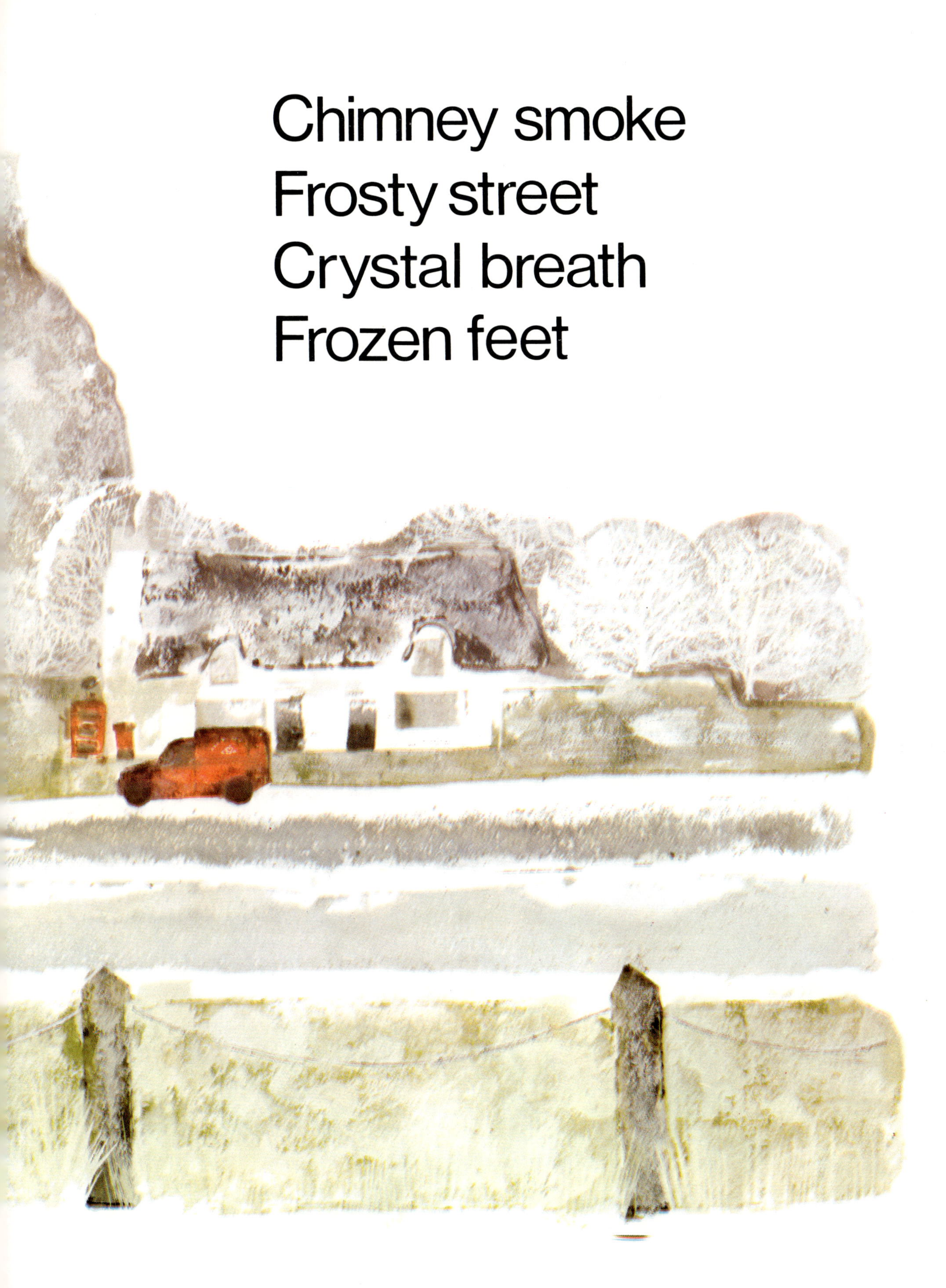

Children calling
Almost nine
School beginning
Daytime